BRITISH HISTORY

Early Britain

500,000 BC-AD 1154

KING*f*ISHER

KINGFISHER
Kingfisher Publications Plc
New Penderel House, 283–288 High Holborn
London WC1V 7HZ
www.kingfisherpub.com

Material in this edition previously published by Kingfisher Publications Plc
in *Children's Illustrated Encyclopedia of British History* in 1992

This revised, reformatted and updated edition published by
Kingfisher Publications Plc in 2002

1TR/0202/PROSP/RNB/140MA

2 4 6 8 10 9 7 5 3 1

A CIP catalogue record for this book is available from the British Library

ISBN 0 7534 0097 9

Printed in China

Consultants: Dr Paul Bahn, David Haycock,
Susan Morris and Valerie St Johnston
Editor: James Harrison, with
Jean Coppendale and Honor Head
Designer: Edward Kinsey
Picture researchers: Alex Goldberg, Elaine Willis
Indexer: Sylvia Potter
Cover design: Mike Davis

CONTENTS

EARLY BRITAIN
(c. 500,000 BC – AD 440)

THE EARLY STORY OF BRITAIN starts some half a million years ago in prehistory (the vast period of time before written records). The earliest people hunted animals and gathered food from what was around them. These hunters and gatherers began to build camps some of which have been discovered. From the stone tools and other remains found at these sites we can learn what life was like before recorded history. Later hunters discovered how to make and use metals such as bronze and copper, and also started to keep sheep and cattle – the first farmers. They built primitive villages and dug huge ditches to make hill forts. At about the time the Egyptians were building the Great Pyramid of Giza, the earliest Britons started to build Stonehenge (*below*) – one of the most remarkable prehistoric stone structures in the world. Britain was still a fairly primitive land compared with Egypt and other major civilizations. By about 500 BC, however, Celtic tribes had settled in Britain and were making iron weapons and utensils, using wheeled carts and chariots and building impressive hill-forts such as Maiden Castle in Dorset.

Stonehenge may have been laid out to mark the position of the midsummer sunrise.

Early Britain

THE EARLIEST HISTORY OF BRITAIN starts in the period known as prehistory, before writing was invented. In Britain, the first written records were introduced by the Romans, so anything that happened in Britain before the Roman Conquest in 55 BC is prehistory.

THE OLD STONE AGE

Archaeologists, people who dig up and examine the remains of prehistory and later periods of history, have discovered two open-air camps near Clacton-on-Sea in Essex and Boxgrove in Sussex. Both sites contain human and animal bones and masses of stone tools. The earliest people lived on this land as long ago as 500,000 years in what is called the Old Stone Age.

In these prehistoric times, there were four great Ice Ages when much of the land was covered by thick ice sheets. In the warmer spells the ice retreated and Old Stone Age people roamed over tundra. Britain was joined to France by open grasslands over what is now the English Channel. People sheltered in caves, and in tents made from animal skin, and they could make fires – which helped them to survive the harsh conditions.

Above **A flint axe from the Old Stone Age, about a quarter of its real size. Early inhabitants also made flint-tipped spears.**

Right: **In the Ice Age Britain was covered by ice north of the Thames estuary (*see dotted line on map*). The land was also joined to Europe across the Channel (*see area shaded in green*).**

HUNTER-GATHERERS

At a place called Swanscombe, in Kent, archaeologists have discovered the remains of a young woman who lived almost 200,000 years ago. She was one of the prehistoric people known as hunter-gatherers. They used sharp stone tools and hand-axes to hunt and fish, but they did not yet domesticate, or tame, animals such as the reindeer and horses which surrounded them. They gathered and ate wild berries, nuts, fruit and roots but did not cultivate, or grow anything. Their stone flake tools and axes have been discovered by archaeologists in many parts of Britain and can been seen today in museums around the country.

The Old Stone Age people lived in small family groups of a dozen or so, and used flint tools to scrape reindeer, mammoth and other animal skins and to bore holes into them. They sewed these hides into clothes using animal tissue threaded on bone needles.

TIME CHART
Note: Dates are approximate

● **500,000 to 4500 BC** Old Stone Age (also called Palaeolithic) period

● **500,000 to 300,000 BC** Early people using flint tools near Clacton-on-Sea

● **500,000 BC** Boxgrove open-air camp in Sussex

● **125,000 BC** Last period of glaciation (ice cover) begins

● **40,000 BC** Early people in caves at Creswell Crags, Derbyshire

A NOTE ABOUT DATES
The letters BC indicate the years **B**efore **C**hrist was born; these are placed after the year, and are numbered backwards, so 55 BC (the first Roman invasion), then 54 BC (the second Roman invasion). The letters AD indicate the years after Christ was born (**A**nno **D**omini is Latin for Year of Our Lord.) The letters are placed before the year and are numbered forwards, so AD 410 (when the Romans left Britain) is followed by AD 411.

Left: **Well over 200,000 years ago, Britain's first settlers could make hand-axes using blocks of stones, usually flint.**

Left: **Making fires and sewing animal hides were key activities for early Britons.**

Right: **The first cave paintings and carvings, such as this bison carved in bone, were made in prehistoric times.**

It was the switch to keeping animals and sowing crops, as well as still hunting and fishing for food, that marks the New Stone Age period in Britain.

With farming and settlement came other skills, such as using deer antlers to break the soil for sowing, and making pottery bowls. Some people became flint-miners, using sharp and polished stone axes. The flint mines at Grimes Graves in Norfolk show they could sink shafts over ten metres deep. People also now buried their dead in long burial mounds called barrows which were like chambers. A New Stone Age camp at Windmill Hill in Wiltshire has a group of round barrows. Another site, at Skara Brae in the Orkneys, is claimed to be the oldest village. In the 1920s a storm washed away the sand-hills that had kept it hidden and protected for 5,000 years.

THE NEW STONE AGE

As the ice melted it released more water into the sea until, around 6000 BC, the last land bridge disappeared and Britain was cut off from Europe by the English Channel. But traders and settlers still came to Britain, on boats and rafts. From about 4500 BC the New Stone Age began as people started farming rather more than hunting and gathering for food. Settlers and traders brought seed corn, sheep and cattle with them and, using sharp axeheads fitted onto wooden handles, they cleared the woods around them so their animals could graze and so they could sow crops of wheat and barley. They were the first farmers.

Below: **At Skara Brae in the Orkneys, north of Scotland, you can visit New Stone Age houses built around 3100 BC. They are well preserved, with cupboards and beds** made from slabs of local Orkney stone. The people here wore beads of teeth and bone, made peat fires and kept sheep. The soil was too windswept to grow crops.

● 3200 BC Stonehenge, Wiltshire, begun

● 3100 BC Stone Age village at Skara Brae, Orkney

● 2600 BC Silbury Hill, a huge barrow in Wiltshire, built

● 2500 BC First known British pottery at Windmill Hill, Wiltshire

● 2000 BC First known weaving

● 1900 BC Beaker Folk arrive in Britain, with bronze tools

● 1800 BC Bronze Age begins in Britain

● 800 BC First Celts invade

● 700 BC Iron Age begins in Britain

● 350 BC Celts settle in Ireland

● 200 BC Celts settle in Taymouth and Moray Firth

Above: Stonehenge was built in three stages, beginning about 3200 BC and ending about 1300 BC. Huge standing stones such as these are called megaliths (from the Greek *mega-*, large, and *lith*, stone), and are scattered throughout northern Europe. They may have been used to observe the sun, moon and stars, as well as to record the seasons.

Below: Around 4,000 years ago the first farming villages appeared made of wood and thatched straw. The people grew barley and wheat and learned to spin and weave wool. They also made simple pots from clay.

THE BRONZE AGE

From around 1800 BC, people began to make metal tools and knife-daggers of bronze, by mixing copper with tin over very hot fires. Britain had plenty of tin, copper and even gold. Britain first became known to the classical world of Greece and Rome as the Cassiterides, the Islands of Tin. The island inhabitants continued the New Stone Age way of life, clearing woods to make open land for growing crops and erecting more dwellings.

STONEHENGE AND AVEBURY

These early settlers also built the most spectacular Bronze Age site in Europe, at Stonehenge, on Salisbury Plain in Wiltshire. It includes a ring of 80 massive rocks that were brought from the Prescelly Mountains in southern Wales, a journey of about 390 kilometres. The huge sandstone blocks in the centre were dragged from Avebury, 30 kilometres away. Avebury itself has an even larger henge, or stone circle. Though less well preserved, it is even older than Stonehenge. Passing through Avebury is the Ridgeway, an ancient road just over 150 kilometres long, that can still be travelled.

THE CELTS AND THE IRON AGE

Around 700 BC, the first iron-using tribes, the Celts, arrived from Europe. They knew how to make much stronger iron weapons, nails and tools such as axes and saws. They used sturdy war chariots and armour, and made bronze, rather than flint, sickles for reaping corn. They also made the first bronze musical horns, and gold cups and jewellery. By about 500 BC the first wheeled carts were in use on Britain's ancient routes.

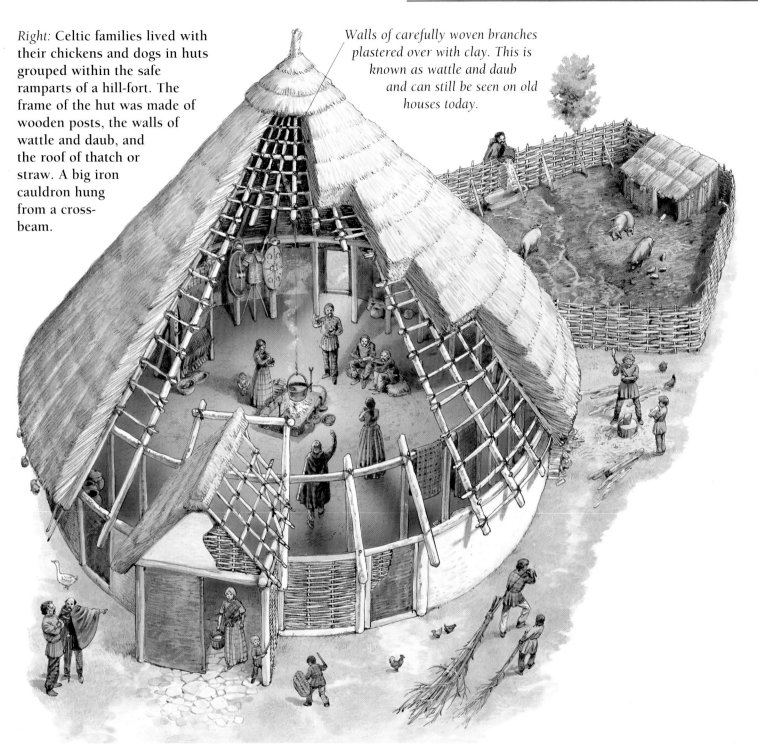

Right: Celtic families lived with their chickens and dogs in huts grouped within the safe ramparts of a hill-fort. The frame of the hut was made of wooden posts, the walls of wattle and daub, and the roof of thatch or straw. A big iron cauldron hung from a cross-beam.

Walls of carefully woven branches plastered over with clay. This is known as wattle and daub and can still be seen on old houses today.

The Celtic tribes who settled in Britain, and their descendants, are called Britons. Their language is still spoken today, because Welsh, Gaelic, Irish and Cornish are directly related to Celtic. For example, the Celtic word for river is *avon*. The Celts left no written records themselves, but the Romans wrote about them, and their first accounts of these islands tell of Celtic life in Britain.

These Iron Age Britons built great hill-forts, the best known of which is Maiden Castle in Dorset. They were built on high ground with commanding views of the surrounding countryside, and were made of rock and earth dug out of the ground with very deep and steep-sided slopes. Inside were enough circular thatched dwellings to make up a small town. Tribal life was dominated by the chieftains, their warriors, and by priests called druids.

Although the Celts conquered much of Europe, their power was eventually threatened by the well-organized armies of the Roman empire.

5

The Romans

BY 100 BC THE ROMANS had an empire that bordered all of the Mediterranean Sea, and stretched across most of Europe, North Africa and the Middle East up to the Red Sea. The Roman army's legions had conquered France, which was called Gaul, and were poised to cross the English Channel. Their knowledge of Britain came from the reports of traders. At first, invasion was not considered worthwhile because the goods the island had to offer – tin, cloth, corn, gold and slaves – could be taken from other tribes on the Continent. But army commanders, including Julius Caesar, the governor of Gaul, wanted more victories. He was troubled by Celtic revolts which had support from tribes in the south of Britain.

ROMAN INVASIONS

Julius Caesar landed on the English coast, probably at Deal, near Dover, Kent, in 55 BC. Although he had 10,000 troops and cavalry, storms damaged his ships and after fierce fighting with the Britons he had to retreat. In 54 BC, the Romans made a second invasion, moving inland and taking the hill-fort of Bigbury, near Canterbury. The British tribes were now under one chief, Cassivellaunus of the Catuvellauni tribe, whose base was north of the River Thames near modern-day St Albans. Caesar's well-organized Roman troops crossed the River Medway, then the Thames, and forced the Britons to submit to him.

But revolt in Gaul and civil war in Rome took Caesar and his army away, never to return. The Catuvellauni grew strong again under their chief Cunobelinus. For the next 100 years they controlled the southeast with their capital at Camulodunum, now Colchester, in Essex.

- **75 BC** Catuvellauni tribe (from present-day Belgium) settle at Colchester
- **55 BC** Julius Caesar invades Britain near Dover, but has to retreat
- **54 BC** Caesar raids again with five legions and reaches Essex
- *c.* **5 BC** Birth of Jesus Christ
- *c.* **AD 30** Crucifixion of Jesus
- **AD 43** Four Roman legions under Aulus Plautius invade Britain
- **AD 44** Emperor Claudius arrives in Britain and captures Camulodunum (Colchester)
- **AD 45** Vespasian (later emperor) captures Vectis (the Isle of Wight)
- **AD 47** Ostorius Scapula defeats the Iceni in East Anglia
- **AD 48** Romans begin conquest of Wales
- **AD 51** Caractacus (Caradog), King of the Silures, is captured and taken to Rome

Above: **A Roman soldier with shield, spear, short stabbing sword and light armour. In total he carried about 30 kg of equipment.**

Below: **Roman soldiers fought in groups called legions, fighting in formation with swords and spears and protecting themselves with shields.**

ROMAN RULE

In AD 43, the Emperor Claudius sent 40,000 troops under the command of Aulus Plautius, to conquer Britain. Claudius came the next year and entered Camulodunum (Colchester) in triumph. Caractacus led the British resistance for the next seven years. He was eventually handed over to the Romans by Queen Cartimandua of the Brigantes, a northern tribe, who had signed a treaty with the Romans when he fled to her for refuge. Caractacus was led through the streets of Rome bound in chains.

BOUDICCA'S REVOLT

In AD 60 Prasutagus, King of the Iceni, a Norfolk tribe, died and left his fortune jointly to his two daughters and the Roman emperor. The Romans proceeded to take over the kingdom, and Catus, the Roman treasurer, seized all of the king's dominions, ill-treated the daughters and had their mother, Queen Boudicca, publicly bound and scourged. Outraged, Boudicca led a fierce revolt. Under her leadership the Iceni burned Camulodunum (Colchester), Verulamium (St Albans) and Londinium (London) and slaughtered many Romans. The Romans rallied under their governor and defeated Boudicca, who killed herself. Organized resistance by British tribes to Rome was over.

Britain was now the furthest northwest province of the Roman empire. The Romans needed to protect the valuable British minerals such as tin, iron ore, gold and lead. Roman troops went as far as Exeter in Devon, and to the coast and valleys of Wales. In 1996 archaeologists reported that they had discovered a Roman fort on the coast of Ireland which shows the Romans might have established a foothold even further west than was previously believed. But the troops could not control what is now Scotland, where they encountered the fierce Pictish, or painted, tribes.

HADRIAN'S WALL

In AD 122 the Emperor Hadrian visited Britain – the first to do so since Claudius – and decided to establish a secure northern frontier for the Roman province. So he ordered a wall to be built across the narrowest part of the country, from the river Tyne to the Solway Firth. Hadrian's Wall, a great work of military engineering, stretched across the country for 117 kilometres.

Above: **Boudicca, Queen of the Iceni (in modern Norfolk) in her war chariot. She headed a great revolt against the Romans but was defeated in AD 62. She took her own life.**

Below: **The Romans left over 9,000 km of straight roads in Britain, including the Fosse Way from Lincoln down into Devon. They also built the famous** Hadrian's Wall, and the not so well known Antonine Wall, made of turf and stretching 60 km from present-day Glasgow to Edinburgh.

Above: **Roman roads were paved with thick slabs of stone and raised in the centre so rainwater ran into ditches at the sides. Many stretches of these roads still exist.**

Below: **The Romans enjoyed public baths and the most famous in Britain are located at Bath in Avon. Aquae Sulis, as Bath was called, fell into Saxon hands in AD 577. Roman baths had 1 an** exercise area (*palaestra*); **2** changing room (*apodyterium*); **3** cool bath (*frigidarium*); **4** warm bath (*tepidarium*); **5** hot room (*caldarium*); **6** underfloor heating system (*hypocaust*).

Hadrian's Wall took seven years to complete, and long stretches of it still stand today at a height of 2 metres. The wall was made of stone about 4.5 metres high and 3 metres thick, with a ditch on the north side. A second ditch, or *vallum*, was later dug to the south. About every 1.5 kilometres stood a small fort called a milecastle – a barracks for between 25 and 50 men. In total, as many as 5,000 troops might have been needed to guard, supply and to look after the entire wall's defences. There were also 17 major forts added to the wall at regular distances. These were really small military towns with headquarters, barracks for the troops to sleep in, workshops for weapons and tools, a hospital and a large granary for food supplies. One fort, at Birdoswald in Cumbria, had 1,000 people.

LIFE IN ROMAN BRITAIN

From AD 70 onwards for 100 years, Britain under Roman rule was peaceful and prosperous. But what other benefits did the Romans bring? Perhaps most importantly they brought a written language, Latin, and written numbers. The history of Britain was now recorded on paper and many of the first accounts have been passed down by Roman writers. The Romans were also highly organized: they introduced a ten month calendar, and fixed hours of the day. They also built a huge network of roads, including Fosse Way and Watling Street.

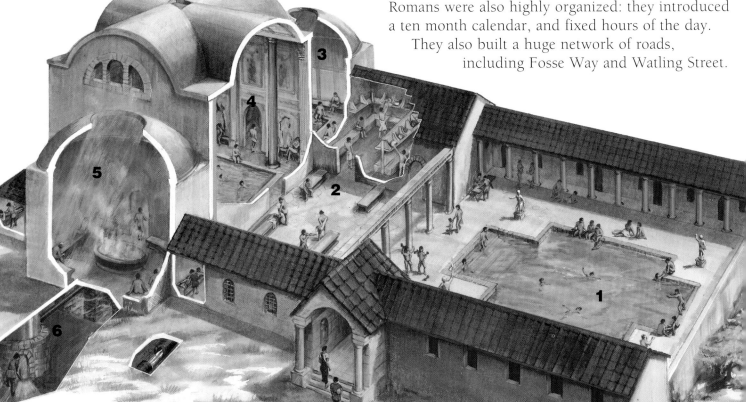

Right: **The important public buildings in Roman towns:**
1 forum (market place);
2 temple; **3** circus (stadium);
4 baths; **5** theatre. The town wall defences had four main gates **6**.

Archaeologists have excavated large numbers of Roman agricultural tools such as hoes, sickles, pruning hooks for fruit trees, and rakes with iron spikes and spades with iron edges. Other Roman remains include blacksmiths' hammers, anvils and furnace bars, as well as pieces of pottery lamps which lit their houses, and decorated jewellery of bronze, glass and gold.

ROMAN TOWN LIFE

The roads were vital military and trade routes in Roman Britain, linking the fortified Roman towns of London, York, Chester, Lincoln and St Albans. The Romans built new towns or converted Celtic bases introducing proper drains and straight streets that intersected one another at right angles like streets in a modern American city. At the centre of the town was the forum or market place, with a basilica or town hall, and a temple and public baths close by.

The public baths were places for people to meet together to gossip, to do sports or discuss business, rather than simply to wash. The baths were cheap and children got in free. The Romans also built theatres and amphitheatres in several British towns such as St Albans. In these huge arenas, a variety of different shows were put on to amuse the people such as gladiators fighting each other to the death, cock-fighting and bull-baiting.

ROMAN COUNTRY LIFE

Many Britons did not change their way of life under Roman rule. In the countryside, they continued to live in round timber-framed houses and farm much as they had done before the invasion, supporting their families. Because life in the countryside was largely unchanged, archaeologists call the inhabitants of Roman Britain Romano-British (rather than Roman) and that is the name given to things they made and built.

An important change in the British countryside was the Roman villa. Not unlike the stately homes of later centuries, these were large, luxurious houses surrounded by a big estate. They often had mosaic floors and painted walls, and some had glass windows. There would be several bedrooms, living rooms and a large kitchen. Some had central heating (*hypocausts*) with hot water running under the floors.

9

Above: **The Chi-Ro mosaic at Lullingstone in Kent shows the Christian sign: two Greek letters Chi and Ro – CHR – which stands for *Christos*, or Christ, in Greek. Christianity was brought to Britain by the Romans.**

- **AD 60** Romans conquer Anglesey, stronghold of the Druids. Revolt of Boudicca

- **AD 81** Julius Agricola reaches the Firth of Forth and establishes northern frontier

- **AD 84** Agricola defeats the Picts in the Highlands

- **AD 123** Emperor Hadrian builds his great wall on Tyne-Solway line

- **AD 143** Romans build Antonine Wall from Firth of Forth to the River Clyde

- **AD 163** Romans withdraw south to Hadrian's Wall

- **AD 208** Emperor Septimius Severus arrives; invades Caledonia (Scotland)

- **AD 211** Severus dies at York

- **AD 280** Saxon pirate raids

- **AD 284** Emperor Diocletian makes Britain part of the Prefecture of Gaul (France)

- **AD 287** St Alban martyred for sheltering a fugitive Christian

- **AD 314** Bishops from Lincoln, London and York attend Council of Arles (assembly of the Church of Rome)

Below: **A Roman coin found at Richborough, in Kent, dated AD 410. A Briton cowers before a fully armed Roman soldier on horseback. Richborough, in Kent, was Julius Caesar's chief port and military base.**

DECLINE OF THE EMPIRE

The Romans had to keep soldiers in Britain all the time to guard it against attack. From about AD 280 onwards, Saxon pirates (from what is now Germany) began raiding the shores of Britain. In the north, at the least sign of weakness in the Roman defence the Picts were ready to pour over Hadrian's Wall.

To guard against the Saxon raids, the Romans built a chain of forts along the shores from Norfolk to the Isle of Wight. The forts were under the command of an officer known as the Count of the Saxon Shore. The forts had massive walls, several of which still stand today. Burgh Castle in Norfolk has a fine example of such a wall. These forts held off the raiders until AD 367 when the Picts, the Saxons and warriors from northern Ireland joined forces. These invaders broke through Hadrian's Wall, and killed the Count of the Saxon Shore. But the Romans gradually restored order and made treaties with some of the northern tribes.

THE END OF ROMAN RULE

Two things combined to bring about the end of Roman rule in Britain. One was civil war between rival generals fighting to become emperor. The other was the increasing number of attacks on Rome by barbarian tribes from northern Europe. Slowly, legions of troops were withdrawn from Britain to protect other parts of the Roman empire. The last legion left in AD 406. Four years later, when the Romano-British appealed for help against other foreign invaders, the emperor could only reply: "Take steps to defend yourselves". Roman coins stopped being used by AD 430; Hadrian's Wall and other forts were neglected and villas abandoned; nobody repaired the roads; and 400 years of Roman rule in Britain slowly disappeared.

ROMAN CHRISTIANITY

Christianity was probably brought to Britain by Roman soldiers or civilian settlers from Gaul some time before AD 200. The influence of Roman Christianity led to the building of crosses and later churches. Saxon and British pagan gods and goddesses were slowly replaced. In AD 287 Alban, a Romano-Briton living at Verulamium, sheltered a Christian fleeing from persecution, and was put to death. (Verulamium is now known by its present name of St Albans.)

The Emperor Constantine made Christianity Rome's official religion in AD 324, by which time England already had three bishops, at Lincoln, London and York.

Left: A Roman pot made in about AD 200 shows men fighting. One holds up a finger to show he has lost. Some pots were made of bronze or iron and others of terracotta (clay). Most pottery was made for table use as platters, bowls or drinking cups.

ST PATRICK AND THE IRISH

Ireland's first great leader was Cormac, who ruled over Meath and Connacht from AD 275 to 300. He made himself *Ard-Rí* (high king), and set up a national assembly at Tara Hill, in Meath. Even more powerful was Niall of the Nine Hostages, who was high king from AD 380 to 405. At around this time a 16-year-old Romano-British boy, Patrick, was carried off to pagan Ireland and made a slave. He escaped and trained as a Christian priest. About 30 years later he went back to Ireland as a bishop and a missionary. There were already a few Christians in Ireland, but Patrick's preaching converted almost all the island. Many legends grew up about Patrick, for instance he is supposed to have banished all the snakes from Ireland. (In fact snakes never reached Ireland after the Ice Age. Ireland became an island at a time when Britain was still attached to the European mainland.) Patrick is the patron saint of Ireland.

Left: The empire is dismantled. The Romans left in AD 406 and the Romano-British abandoned their country villas. Local farmers took away the valuable materials.

- AD **324** Christianity becomes official religion of Roman empire

- AD **325** British bishops attend Council of Nicaea, first world-wide council of Christian Church

- AD **366** Picts raid as far south as London

- AD **367** Roman general Theodosius drives the Picts north beyond Hadrian's Wall

- AD **401** St Patrick sold into slavery in Ireland by pirates

- AD **406** Last Roman legion leaves Britain

- AD **407** Romano-Briton Constantine proclaims himself emperor

- AD **410** Emperor Honorius tells Romano-Britons that Rome can no longer defend them

The Anglo-Saxons were skilled metal workers, as this beautifully finished gold shoulder clasp shows.

THE ANGLO-SAXONS
(440 – 1066)

THE ROMAN EMPIRE SPLIT in two – the Western Roman empire and the Eastern (Byzantine) empire. In AD 476 the Western Roman empire collapsed, and the years after this are often known as the Dark Ages. This is partly because so little is known about what happened at that time, and partly because the end of Roman law and order also led to the loss of classical culture, science and learning. The Dark Ages began in Britain much earlier than in the rest of Europe, when the last of the Roman legions left in AD 406. The soldiers were recalled to defend their empire, which was under threat from barbarian invasion, and they were never to return.

By that time Britain was already being attacked by Saxon pirates. The attacks grew stronger and more frequent. For a time the Romano-British people fought them off. Stories of that grim struggle are contained in the legends of King Arthur. But it was the pirate raiders who eventually won. Saxons, Jutes and Angles invaded Britain from northern Germany. From the Angles comes the word Angleland – England.

Later invaders were the Northmen, the fierce Vikings who settled in northern and eastern England and left their mark in place names containing old Norse words like *by*, a village, or *thwaite*, a clearing.

The Anglo-Saxons

EVEN BEFORE THE ROMANS left Britain in AD 406, England was being raided by Saxon pirates as well as by Jutes and Angles attacking from northern Germany, Denmark and what is now Holland and Belgium. The Picts from Scotland also broke through Hadrian's Wall and raided England.

Some Romano-British chiefs fought off these raiders with their own armies. But others invited mercenaries (paid soldiers) to help them fight their enemies. According to legend, the first German mercenaries to come to Britain and wage war on the Romano-British were Hengist and Horsa. The Anglo-Saxons (as we call the Saxons, Angles and Jutes) drove off the Picts, but instead of going back to their homeland they took over the Romano-British kingdoms by force.

- ● **450** Treasure buried at Mildenhall, Suffolk (found 1942)

- ● **476** Goths conquer Rome: end of Western Roman empire

- ● **477** Saxons arrive in England in force

- ● *c.* **500** Saxons defeated at Badon Hill by Britons under King Arthur

Below: **This map shows the borders of the various Anglo-Saxon tribes in England after the fall of the Roman empire. The Romano-Britons fled to Cornwall, while Wales and most of Scotland remained independent.**

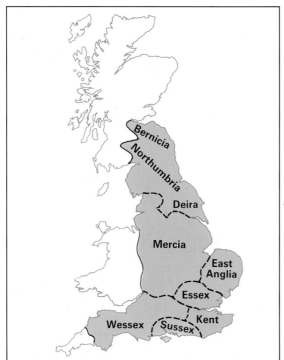

Bernicia
Northumbria
Deira
Mercia
East Anglia
Essex
Wessex
Sussex
Kent

THE DARK AGES AND KING ARTHUR

The years following the collapse of the Roman empire in AD 476 are often known as the Dark Ages, partly because there is so little written history of the time to shed any light on what happened in this period. In many ways it was like a return to life in the Iron Age, before organized Roman rule.

At the time of the fall of the Roman empire there was certainly a Romano-British tribe leader called Arthur who fought the Saxons from about 470 to 500. He lived in a castle called Camelot (it may have been in south Somerset) and he was probably a *dux bellorum*, or commander-in-chief of an army. His most famous victory was at Badon Hill. But the legends of Merlin the magician, the sword Excalibur, Guinevere, Lancelot and the Knights of the Round Table are exciting stories but not history. The Round Table at the Great Hall in Winchester is a Tudor reconstruction.

LIFE UNDER THE ANGLO-SAXONS

The Anglo-Saxons built simple wooden houses and barns and made towns into centres for trade and manufacturing. Craftworkers made pottery and glass, and metal workers included skilled jewellers. Most people were farmers, growing barley, oats and wheat for food, and flax for making linen for clothing. Sheep were kept for their wool as much as for their meat, and the Saxons also kept cattle, pigs and goats.

Under each tribal king there were three classes: noblemen; churls, who were freemen or yeomen, many of them owning land; and slaves. A slave could be bought for the price of eight oxen.

Left: **This is a picture for the month of March from an Anglo-Saxon calendar showing the Saxons working the land.**

From about 450 to 650 the Saxons created new kingdoms such as East Anglia (the kingdom of the East Angles), Kent, Sussex, Wessex, Northumbria and Mercia (present-day Midlands). The ancient Britons fled to Cornwall and Brittany in northern France (from where this region gets its name). Mercia was ruled by King Offa from 757 to 796. A strong ruler with a strong army, he is best known for Offa's Dyke, a defence stretching from the Severn estuary to the Irish Sea to keep out the Welsh. Almost 180 kilometres of earthworks 1.5 metres deep were built with wooden barriers and forts at the top. It can still be seen today. The Anglo-Saxons spoke Old English, which has developed into present-day English.

CELTIC AND ROMAN CHRISTIANS

The Romano-Britons were Christians whereas the Anglo-Saxons were pagans who worshipped their own gods and goddesses. St Patrick's followers Columba and Aidan converted the Anglo-Saxons after the Romans had left. They brought Christianity to Scotland and the north of England. There are Celtic monasteries at Iona in Argyll, Scotland and at Lindisfarne on Holy Island off the Northumberland coast. At Tintagel, Cornwall, lies the oldest known monastery in Britain, built by Celtic Christian monks in 470. In 597 Augustine, a missionary sent from Rome by Pope Gregory I to convert England, arrived in Kent and set up a Roman Christian church at Canterbury, where the cathedral would be built.

During the Dark Ages, Celtic and Roman Christians argued fiercely about the form their Church should take. In 664 King Oswy of Northumbria, who had supported Aidan, called a synod (conference) at Whitby, in Yorkshire. There the Celtic Church leaders under the Abbess Hilda decided to follow the Church of Rome and accept the Pope as their leader like the rest of Europe. They also decided the date of Easter and issues such as the style of a monk's haircut.

Left: **When Saxon soldiers reported that it was safe to land in Britain, whole families arrived. They beached their boats and waded ashore with their sheep and cattle.**

Above: **This elaborate Saxon helmet was crafted of iron, bronze and silver in about 625. It may have belonged to a king of the East Angles.**

15

MONKS AND LEARNING

Much of what we know about Britain comes from the writings of monks. One of the most important sources is the *History of the English Church and People*, completed in Latin in 731 by the Venerable Bede. He was a monk at the great monastery of Jarrow, near Newcastle, where he taught and wrote. Because he set up a school there for 600 monks, he is referred to as the father of English learning. Bede's *History of the English Church and People* was later translated into Anglo-Saxon by Alfred the Great.

In the monastery of Whitby, Caedmon, a monk who was perhaps the first English (or Saxon) poet, wrote *The Creation*, the earliest surviving English poem. Caedmon is thought of as the founder of English poetry. The other major work of this time is the *Anglo-Saxon Chronicle*, begun in the 800s by monks at Winchester, who recorded important events in England in the Anglo-Saxon language.

THE VIKINGS ATTACK

In the late 700s Northmen, or Norsemen, pirates from Scandinavia, began attacking the Anglo-Saxons. These Northmen were known as Vikings, from a Norse word meaning pirate or sea raider. The monks who wrote the *Anglo-Saxon Chronicle* called them "the heathen" or "the force".

The Vikings sailed in longships, sleek and fast all-weather vessels. They were disciplined fighters, but in their raids they slaughtered, burned and robbed. They carried off the most beautiful women, and took men to sell as slaves. They conquered Northumbria, East Anglia and Mercia. Only Wessex held out against them.

KENNETH MACALPIN, KING OF THE SCOTS

The early inhabitants of Scotland formed a number of tribes. By the 600s these tribes had united to form two kingdoms: Pictavia (land of the Picts), who occupied most of the northern part; and Dalriada (land of the Scots), who had moved to Scotland from Ireland.

In 843 Kenneth MacAlpin (son of Alpin), King of the Scots, claimed the throne of Pictavia through his grandmother, who was a Pictish princess. From his time onwards all the land north of the Clyde-Forth line was united and is now Scotland.

Right: **In the Dark Ages, monks were the only scholars. They copied books to send to other monasteries.**

KING EGBERT

During this time, a new dynasty of rulers was begun by Egbert, King of Wessex, who reigned from 802 to 839. He became the first king who could claim to be ruler over all England. Egbert enlarged Wessex (which at this point consisted of Berkshire, Devon, Dorset, Hampshire, Somerset, Wiltshire) to include Kent, Sussex, Surrey and Cornwall.

Egbert defeated Offa's powerful kingdom of Mercia at the battle of Ellandun in 825 (at Wroughton in Wiltshire). After this victory the people of Mercia and Northumbria acknowledged Egbert as Bretwalda (Lord of Britain). Egbert's grandson was Alfred the Great.

ALFRED THE GREAT

The Vikings who invaded England in the mid-800s came from Denmark, so we also call them Danes. They conquered Northumbria, took York and East Anglia, and overran Mercia. They would have conquered the whole of England but for the efforts of Alfred the Great. Alfred was the youngest son of King Ethelwulf of Wessex. He had spent much of his youth in Rome where he was educated.

Above: **Egbert (775-839). After being banished for laying claim to the West Saxon kingship, Egbert later returned to become King of Wessex in 802, and first ruler of England.**

Below: **The Vikings, or Danes, were bold sailors and fearsome soldiers. Their main weapons were swords, axes and spears.**

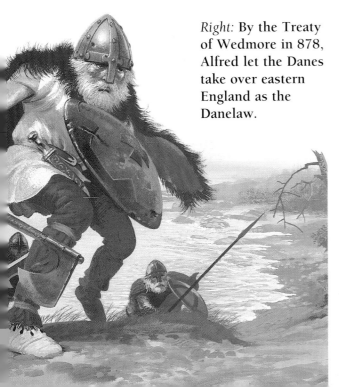

ALFRED DEFEATS THE DANES

During his fierce resistence of the Danes, Alfred spent some months hiding in the Isle of Athelney, among the marshes of Somerset. It is from here that the legend arose of Alfred burning cakes and being scolded by a local swineherd who did not recognize him as king.

In 871 Alfred defeated the Danes at the battle of Ashdown on the Berkshire Downs. He sought a peace in which the Danes agreed not to attack Wessex in return for a payment called the Danegeld – meaning gold for the Danes. But after five years the Danes under King Guthrum again attacked Wessex. Alfred raised an army and defeated the Danes at the battle of Edington in Wiltshire in 878. He also forced the King Guthrum to sign the Treaty of Wedmore and be baptized.

THE DANELAW

A new frontier between Wessex and the Danish territory followed the line of Watling Street, the old Roman road which ran from London to Chester. Alfred allowed the Danes to settle in the lands to the east of Watling Street, in what was later called the Danelaw. The Danes have left us their words such as *loft* as in Lowestoft meaning farmhouse and *thorpe* as in Scunthorpe which means village. In 890, Alfred built a fleet of ships to defend the shores of his southern kingdom of England. He also founded several new fortified towns, called *burhs*.

Right: **By the Treaty of Wedmore in 878, Alfred let the Danes take over eastern England as the Danelaw.**

Danelaw

English Mercia

Wessex

- **540** Bubonic plague in Britain
- **563** St Columba founds Iona monastery in western Scotland
- **590** Gregory I, the Great, becomes Pope (to 604)
- **597** St Augustine founds a monastery at Canterbury
- **600** Saxons, Angles and Jutes control most of England
- **604** First church of St Paul, London
- **613** Northumbrians defeat Britons near Chester
- **624-625** Sutton Hoo ship burial
- **627** Bishop Paulinus converts Edwin of Northumbria to Christianity and becomes Archbishop of York
- **635** Lindisfarne monastery established. St Aidan Bishop of Northumbria
- **642** Oswald of Northumbria killed in battle against Penda of Mercia
- **650** Epic poem *Beowulf* written
- **664** Synod of Whitby: Roman form of worship chosen over Celtic
- **704** Ethelred of Mercia abdicates to become a monk
- **716** Ethelbald becomes King of Mercia (to 747)
- **731** Venerable Bede completes *History of the English Church and People*
- **750** Gregorian chants first sung in England
- **757** Offa becomes King of Mercia (to 796)
- **760** *Book of Kells* written in Ireland
- **772-775** Offa builds Offa's Dyke defence to keep out the Welsh

Left: The Alfred Jewel, set in gold and crystal with a miniature enamel portrait of the king. It has the Saxon words for "Alfred ordered me to be made". This may have been the decorated end of a bookmark, to be used by a priest or monk when reading the Bible. Alfred was a religious man and encouraged his people to go to church.

- **787** Vikings raid Wessex

- **794** Vikings raid Scottish isles

- **795** First Viking raid on Ireland

- **802** Egbert is King of Wessex (to 839); Mercia's dominance is challenged

- **834** Kenneth MacAlpin becomes King of the Scots

- **843** MacAlpin defeats the Picts and unites Picts and Scots

- **856** Ethelwulf dies; succeeded by Ethelbald (to 860), Ethelbert (to 865) and Ethelred (to 871)

- **869** Danes occupy East Anglia and kill St Edmund

- **871** Alfred the Great becomes King of Wessex (to 899)

- **878** Alfred defeats Danes; Treaty of Wedmore divides England between Danes (Danelaw) and Saxons

- **890** Alfred establishes navy

- **891** *Anglo-Saxon Chronicle* begun

- **900** England divided into shires

- **919** Danes triumph in Dublin

- **980** Danes begin almost yearly raids on Britain

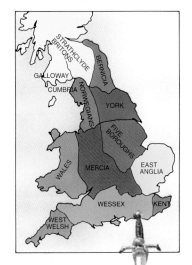

Above: In Alfred the Great's time England was divided into many small kingdoms.

Right: A statue of Alfred the Great stands at Wantage in Oxfordshire, his birthplace. Alfred was devout and scholarly. He translated several works from Latin into Old English.

THE WESSEX KINGS

Three kings, Alfred, Edward the Elder and Athelstan made the Anglo-Saxon kingdom of England strong. Alfred's son, Edward the Elder, defeated the Danes several times in his 25 year reign, and ruled over all England south of the river Humber. The Danelaw settlers of East Anglia and the Midlands submitted to him, and the Welsh princes also acknowledged him as their overlord. Edward's son, Athelstan, defeated a coalition of Vikings, Scots and Irish Celts at the battle of Brunanburh (937).

But a succession of weak rulers lost these gains. The weakest was Ethelred II, who came to the throne in 978, aged ten. Ethelred was known as the *Unraed - redeless*, or evil-counselled. The word was later translated as "unready". The Danes began raiding again and inflicted a defeat over the Saxons at the battle of Maldon in Essex, in 991. Ethelred was ill-advised to use the Danegeld (as Alfred had done at first) to try to buy off the Danes with bribes. Eventually his kingdom shrank to just Wessex and Kent.

Ethelred then attacked the Danes who were living peacefully in Wessex, including Gunhilda, sister of the Danish King Sweyn. Infuriated, the Danes waged war until, in 1013, they proclaimed Sweyn King of England. Ethelred fled to Normandy in France, the home of his wife, Emma. Their marriage established the first dynastic link between England and Normandy.

THE DANISH KINGS

Sweyn died in 1014, one year after becoming King of England. Ethelred came back, but he died in 1016. His son, Edmund Ironside, and Sweyn's son, Canute, battled for the throne. They finally agreed to share the kingdom between them, but Edmund died suddenly, having ruled his portion for just seven months.

Canute now became king of all England. He was also king of much of Scandinavia including Denmark, Norway and southern Sweden, but wisely he chose Englishmen, for the Church and for his Court.

Right: The Danes who moved to Britain were farming people. They lived in simple wooden houses and cleared the forests for land.

KING CANUTE

Canute brought peace and prosperity to England. He supplied a firm, fair government and maintained an army. Canute said: "I have vowed to God to govern my kingdoms with equity, and to act justly in all things". Two of his sons succeeded him as kings from 1035 to 1042: Harold I, known as Harefoot, and Harthacanute. Neither king contributed to the country's development.

THE LAST SAXON KINGS

In 1042, Edward, son of Ethelred II and Emma of Normandy, became king. Although he was a Saxon he had been brought up in Normandy and learned Norman ways. He was so devout that his people called him Edward the Confessor. Westminster Abbey was begun during his reign in 1052. Edward died in 1066 after naming his brother-in-law Harold Godwinsson, Earl of Wessex, as his heir. The Witan, the Saxon council, agreed and he was crowned Harold II at Westminster Abbey on January 6, 1066, the last Saxon king of England.

Left: Edward the Confessor (1042-1066) elder son of Ethelred the Unready and Emma, daughter of Richard, Duke of the Normans. Edward founded Westminster Abbey.

Above: King Canute was surrounded by courtiers who tried to win his favour by flattery. There is a story that, to prove he was not taken in by their flattery, he commanded the tide to turn back – and got wet. Clearly even a king was less powerful than God and the forces of nature.

- **1005** Malcolm II becomes King of Scotland (to 1034)

- **1013** Danes control England. Sweyn proclaimed King of England

- **1016** Canute, son of Sweyn becomes King of England

- **1034** Duncan I is King of Scotland

- **1035** Canute dies; succeeded by son, Harold I (Harefoot)

- **1040** Harold I dies; succeeded by half brother Harthacanute (to 1042). Macbeth kills Duncan I in battle, and becomes King of Scotland (to 1057)

- **1042** Edward, Ethelred II's son, becomes king (to 1066)

- **1057-1058** Duncan's son Malcolm kills Macbeth, and becomes Malcolm III King of Scots

- **1064** Harold Godwinsson shipwrecked in Normandy; forced to swear allegiance to William, Duke of Normandy, before William will release him

- **1066** Edward dies; Harold Godwinsson crowned last Saxon king of England

A beautiful book cover drawn by monks at Kells in Ireland. At the time of the Norman invasion, these monks lived in a monastery with beehive-shaped huts, a central stone chapel and a five-storey round tower.

THE NORMANS

(1066 – 1154)

IN THE 600 YEARS SINCE the Saxon pirates began to settle amid the ruins of the old Roman province of Britain, their descendants had made England one of the wealthiest and best-governed lands in western Europe. The Danes had also finally settled peacefully in the country. All was about to change, however, because the Anglo-Saxon king, Edward the Confessor, had no son to take his place. The storm clouds were gathering. Once again the Northmen threatened. Harald Hardrada of Norway, aided by Tostig, the renegade Earl of Northumbria, was waiting to pounce. So too were William, Duke of Normandy, who was Edward's brother-in-law, and named heir Harold Godwinsson, Earl of Wessex, who was Tostig's brother.

William won the contest, and for the next hundred years England was ruled by Norman kings. The Normans brought about a major change – they ended England's isolation. Henceforth England was very much a part of Europe. Indeed, until 1558, English monarchs owned a part of France – at times the major part.

Scotland and Ireland retained their independence under the Norman kings. Wales already had links with the Saxon kings, and within a few years the Normans overran southern Wales. But for centuries northern Wales remained independent of the Normans.

The Normans

THE NORMANS WERE originally Vikings who had settled in northwest France in the early 900s, by the River Seine. In 1066 an army of up to 7,000 men crossed over the English Channel in hundreds of boats.

CONTENDERS FOR THE CROWN

This invasion was led by William, Duke of Normandy, who claimed that he was the rightful King of England, even though Harold Godwinsson had already been crowned king and accepted by the Witan. King Harold led the English army to oppose the Norman invasion. But he and many of his men were weary. Three weeks earlier they had fought and beaten Harald Hardrada, a Norwegian contender for the throne, at Stamford Bridge in Yorkshire, and then had a six-day forced march back to London. Now Harold's forces assembled on the Sussex downs, near the town of Battle.

Above: **The charge of the Normans at the battle of Hastings. The Normans were more heavily armed than their Saxon opponents.**

Below: **Part of the famous Bayeux Tapestry telling the story of William's conquest. The pictures are embroidered in different coloured wool.**

Left: **William I, the Conqueror (1066-1087) was the illegitimate son of Robert, Duke of Normandy. He defeated Harold, King of England, at the battle of Hastings in 1066 and was crowned king. He was a stern but efficient ruler.**

- **1066** Edward the Confessor dies; Witan offers throne to Harold II; Tostig and Harald Hardrada of Norway invade northern England; defeated at Stamford Bridge by Harold. William of Normandy invades Sussex; defeats and kills Harold at Hastings. Halley's Comet seen

- **1070** Malcolm III invades Northumbria. Lanfranc Archbishop of Canterbury. Hereward the Wake heads a rising in fen country

- **1071** William I subdues fen rebellion

- **1072** William raids Scotland. Normans conquer Sicily in the Mediterranean

- **1073** Lincoln Cathedral begun

- **1078** Tower of London begun. Pope Gregory VII sends legates to reorganize Church in England

- **1079** William's son Robert Curthose begins castle that gives Newcastle-upon-Tyne its name

- **1086** Domesday Book completed

- **1087** William dies at Rouen. William II becomes king. Robert becomes Duke of Normandy

THE BATTLE OF HASTINGS

The Saxons and Normans were closely matched because the battle of Hastings lasted eight hours, a long time for a medieval battle. The best-armed Saxons (the *thegns* and king's bodyguards) formed a shield-wall against the Norman knights and infantry. The opposing armies met at Hastings on October 14, 1066. The English fought on foot with Harold fighting between his two brothers. They fought off several attacks by Normans on horseback. The Normans then pretended to retreat and some of Harold's forces, thinking they had won the battle, chased after them breaking up their shield-wall. Norman archers then fired arrows over them with deadly effect. According to legend, Harold was pierced through the eye by a Norman arrow, and killed.

William of Normandy advanced to Dover, then to Coventry and finally to London. On Christmas Day 1066, he was crowned King of England.

WILLIAM THE CONQUEROR

The man who overthrew the Saxons, and known ever since as William the Conqueror, was the illegitimate son of Duke Robert of Normandy and a tanner's daughter, Arlette. William was only seven when Robert died. Life was hard for any young boy expected to be a duke. It was much worse for a son born out of marriage. By the time he was 20, William had put down one major rebellion by his barons, and he would have to overcome many more.

THE DOMESDAY BOOK

William subdued England by taking the land away from the Anglo-Saxon lords and giving it to his Norman barons. He ordered many wooden and later stone castles to be built to protect his rule, and also sent out men to record what was in his new kingdom. The survey, recorded in the Domesday Book, was carried out in the first seven months of 1086 and showed that the population was about one and a half million. Every manor and land holding was recorded. William could now check that none of his noblemen had seized other property, and exactly what rents and fees their land should bear. Domesday comes from the word *dom*, meaning assessment. It was so thorough that, as the monks of the *Anglo-Saxon Chronicle* commented: "There was not a single hide nor rod of land ... not an ox, a cow, a pig was left out".

Left: The Domesday Book is normally associated with Winchester where it was most probably compiled. It was actually two books: the first volume of 382 pages describes most of the country while the second volume was called Little Domesday, and was possibly compiled by monks at Ely.

FOCUS ON NORMAN CATHEDRALS

The Normans brought over their architects from the Continent, who helped plan big Romanesque churches and cathedrals such as at Chichester and Durham. Romanesque was a style of western European architecture from the 10th to 13th centuries which featured ribbed vaulting and rounded arches. Deep doorways had rounded arches supported on thick, strong pillars and with highly decorated mouldings. The windows were often bordered with a chevron or a V-shape. Norman builders had only simple equipment with which to build their great cathedrals and churches, but the results were spectacular.

Domesday Village Life

VILLAGE LIFE revolved around the parish church because it was the only public building. The church and churchyard were used for fairs and games as well as for religious services and festivals such as Christmas, Whitsun and Easter. Sundays and Mondays were usually days of rest.

Most village people were *villeins*, who owned a few plough oxen and a small piece of land called a small-holding. They had to farm on the lord of the manor's land for certain amounts of time, and then at other times they could cultivate their own strips of land and tend to their livestock. Below villeins were the *bordars* who owned even less land (about two hectares) and had no livestock.

There were often one or two manors in a village and the barons owned all the large open fields, with some of the peasants being allowed to own much smaller strips of land. Any meadow or woodland was also owned by the barons. Manors varied greatly in size, ranging from many square kilometres to just a few hectares.

Farming was mainly hard manual work – sowing, weeding and harvesting were all done by hand. Only ploughing was aided by oxen. Sheep were the most important livestock, and often those belonging to villagers outnumbered those owned by the manor. Sheep were raised for their meat, for their wool (which could be sold by the owners), and for cheese made from their milk. At harvest time the lord of the manor would

Right: **An artist's impression of what a typical baron's manor would have looked like. The manor was a fortified home and it would have included a castle 1 for a lookout and protection. The baron himself would have lived in the large thatched building 2 inside a defensive picket fence called a bailey 3. The farm buildings 4 include barns, a blacksmith's shop and the bailiff's (farm manager) house. The villeins' houses 5 are grouped away from the baron's castle, around the parish church 6. There are three fields for farming: one for wheat 7, one for barley or oats 8 and one left fallow 9. This baron also has a deer park 10, a vineyard 11, and an orchard 12.**

provide pork, chicken, cabbages, eggs, cheese and apples for those gathering the crops.

In the autumn many farm animals were killed and their meat preserved in salt. This saved on precious winter fodder and also meant the villagers had a source of nourishment during the long winter months. They ate fish on Fridays and Holy Days as the Church did not allow them to eat meat on these days. The manor also ran the water-mill for grinding the manor's and the villagers' corn. There were also fisheries on the rivers, with part of the catch paid to the lord of the manor. Hunting was reserved for the Norman lords who created areas of countryside in which deer and boars could roam.

Above: A house belonging to a tenant called a bordar. He was one of the lowest tenants in the feudal structure of land ownership and loyalty to the lord of the manor. This house has a timber frame filled in with wattle and daub (which is mud and plaster on a wicker mesh). It is built close to a wood and would have a run for pigs reared in the woods and fed on acorns. After sheep, pigs were the most important livestock, and the Domesday Book often described woods by the number of pigs that could be kept in them. Women worked as hard in the village as men, helping them in the fields, making baskets, plucking geese for arrow-feathers, stitching sheepskin for saddle-bags and churning butter – all duties performed for the manor house. At home, women would look after their children, house and garden.

The Feudal System

UNDER WHAT IS CALLED the feudal system, which the Normans brought with them from France, all the land in England was owned by the king. He allowed others to hold some of it in return for certain services. The Domesday Book reveals what was owned by the king and through him, by his barons. These barons had private armies, under the command of knights, who were meant to be ready to fight for the king whenever he wanted them to do so. The barons built castles for defence and lived in manor houses.

HOW FEUDALISM BEGAN

After the collapse of the Roman empire, around the year AD 476, law and order had crumbled in Europe and barbarians invaded from all sides. The feudal system grew out of this lawlessness. It began in France, in about AD 750, and soon spread across Europe.

Fearing for their lives, people banded together under the protection of strong leaders or kings. But no leader was strong enough on his own to resist attack or control fighting between local barons, so the king granted land to certain powerful barons, in return for their promising to help him fight his enemies and pay him taxes.

HOW THE FEUDAL SYSTEM WORKED

The feudal system was based on exchanging land for services rather than for rent. The term comes from the Latin for fief, *feudum*, which means any land given away. At the top were the barons and Church institutions who held land given to them by the king and were called tenants-in-chief. In return for this land they were expected to pay the king taxes and provide him with knights to help him fight his enemies. William tried to ensure the barons' estates were scattered about the country so their power was diluted.

The barons kept some land for themselves and also allowed their knights to hold some of their land. Knights were trained warriors. In exchange for land, each knight had to promise to follow his baron to war or guard his castle for 40 days in a year, and provide a certain number of soldiers.

Left: William I made all landowners swear loyalty only to him. This meant they could not swear loyalty to powerful barons who might then build up private armies against the king. William also introduced the practice of knight service, whereby each knight had to follow the baron to war or guard his castle, for 40 days each year. In turn, the baron pledged allegiance to the king.

Below the knights in the feudal system came yeomen, or farmers, who were all free men. They usually lived in a village near the manor house and had to work a few days a week for the baron. At the lowest level were the peasants, known as serfs, who provided the baron with crops in return for protection. Serfs belonged to the baron, as property. They could be bought or sold, as could their children. They could not leave the village or get married without the baron's permission. They did not own their land. This series of arrangements was the basis of what is called the feudal system.

Right: The feudal system created a definite hierarchy, from the powerful at the top to the poorest at the bottom. First came the clergy, then the knight and his family, who were loyal to a baron. The middle class of merchants, lawyers, and yeoman farmers did not owe any services to a baron – they were free, as were craftworkers and shopkeepers. At the bottom were footsoldiers and the serfs.

FOCUS ON THE TOWER OF LONDON

As soon as the Normans moved into an area they would build a wooden fort, usually on a high earth mound with the garrison below protected by high wooden ramparts. The site would be carefully chosen because it overlooked the neighbouring countryside or it dominated a river or important overland route.

No castle could be built without the king's permission – another way of keeping the feudal system working and the barons in check. The most famous castle was the White Tower, built in London to protect the city from enemies coming up the Thames. The White Tower started out as a simple timber-and-earth castle built a few months after the victory at Hastings. By 1100 it was a large 28 metre stone tower with rooms for the royal family, surrounded by wooden buildings for the army and administrators. Today, the White Tower is known by its more famous name: the Tower of London – once the main residence for all English kings from William II to Henry VII. It was also to become a royal mint, a prison, a place of execution and home for the Crown Jewels and Royal Armoury. The Royal Armoury was moved to Leeds in 1996.

- **1089** William II campaigns to take Normandy from his brother

- **1090** Most of Wales comes under Norman rule. Ely and Norwich cathedrals begun

- **1092** William takes Cumbria from Scots

- **1093** Anselm of Bec becomes Archbishop of Canterbury. Malcolm III of Scotland killed while invading England: Donald Bane succeeds him. Durham Cathedral begun

- **1094** Revolt in northwest Wales. Duncan II, son of Malcolm III, drives out Donald Bane, but is later killed

- **1095** Anselm quarrels with William and goes to Rome.

- **1096** First Crusade begins. Normans conquer south Wales. William lends Robert funds for a crusade in return for keeping Normandy as a loan

- **1097** Edgar, son of Malcolm III, deposes and succeeds Donald Bane (to 1107); he accepts William as his overlord. Revolt by the Welsh

- **1099** William holds his first court at Westminster. He conquers Maine in north France

- **1100** William II killed while hunting; succeeded by Henry I (to 1135). Henry marries Matilda, daughter of Malcolm III of Scotland

- **1101** Robert of Normandy, back from the crusades, invades England, but is bought off

- **1106** Henry I defeats and captures Robert at battle of Tinchebrai, and gains Normandy

- **1107** Synod of Westminster: Henry gives up his right to choose bishops and abbots, and is reconciled with Anselm

- **1109** Anselm dies. Henry at war with France

WILLIAM II – THE RED KING

William the Conqueror died from injuries he suffered following a riding accident in 1087. He left Normandy to his eldest son, Robert, and England to his younger but more tough-minded son, William. William II was known as Rufus because of his ruddy complexion (Rufus means red in Latin). William II continued his father's strong rule but he was also a cruel king. He taxed his subjects, including the Church, as much as he could. Several times his barons rebelled in support of Robert of Normandy, a gentler man whom they thought would be easier to deal with. William suppressed these revolts with the aid of the *fyrd*, the old Saxon part-time army. He also fought off two invasions from Malcolm III of Scotland. Scotland and Ireland kept their independence under the Norman kings.

William II was fond of hunting stags and while out hunting in the New Forest he was killed by an arrow. It may have been an accident, but some say that Walter Tyrell, who fired the arrow, was acting on orders from William's younger brother, Henry.

Above: **William II, Rufus, (1087-1100) was born in 1066. He had long flame-red hair, and was hated by his people. He was shot by an arrow while hunting in the New Forest.**

Above: **Henry I (1100-1135) was born in 1068. He seized the throne on the death of Rufus. A strong king, it was said that in his time no man dared to harm another.**

Above: **Ten thousand Norman soldiers were stationed throughout England.**

Left: **With some 70 years of Norman rule and relative peace, towns began to grow. Traders and craftworkers settled in the bigger towns, such as London and Winchester.**

HENRY I

Henry seized the throne and took possession of the royal treasury at Winchester the day after William's death. Robert of Normandy did not accept Henry I as king and the two fought on both sides of the Channel until, in 1106, Henry defeated Robert at the battle of Tinchebrai in Normandy. Robert was imprisoned in England for 28 years until his death. Henry I became known as the Lion of Justice.

THE *CURIA REGIS*

King Henry set up the *Curia Regis,* or King's Council to settle land and other disputes between the king and his tenants. This was the beginning of the Civil Service, the body of officials who help the government run the country.

Henry, who was often absent in Normandy, needed an efficient government to operate in England in his absence. He created a class of loyal administrators from the servants of his royal household, including the chamberlain, who looked after the royal bedchamber; the marshal, who controlled the royal stables; the treasurer; and the steward, who looked after Court officials called ushers. Henry's chancellor, or secretary, issued writs for the sheriffs, or shire-reeves, who administered the counties. The chief officer of the state was the justiciar, who was the equivalent of today's Lord Chief Justice, but also acted as regent, or stand-in, when the king was overseas.

Above: **In 1120, the** *White Ship,* **carrying Henry I's son, William, struck some rocks and sank in the English Channel. William was drowned.**

THE *WHITE SHIP* DISASTER

Henry I had made himself popular with his Saxon subjects by marrying Edith (also known as Matilda), the daughter of Malcolm III of Scotland and of Margaret, a Saxon princess, herself sister of Edgar Atheling, a Saxon claimant to the throne. In 1120 Henry I's only son, William, and Henry's daughter Adela, were drowned returning from Normandy to England in a vessel called the *White Ship.* Henry was so grief-stricken that, it is said, he was never again seen to smile.

FOCUS ON NORMAN CRAFTWORKERS

Craftworkers such as stone masons and metal workers lived in the towns and sold their goods there. Stone masons carved stone columns and blocks, as well as decorative gargoyles, sometimes with the faces of people they knew! They carved their own special marks on cathedrals, churches and castles to identify

their work. The main crafts were cloth making, leatherwork, carpentry and metalwork. For hundreds of years wool was the main British export to Europe, where it was dyed in vats and woven into cloth. Goldsmiths were also busy and safehouses were provided to keep their priceless ornaments out of the reach of robbers.

Henry had lost his only legitimate son and heir to the throne, so he now tried to persuade his barons to swear to stand by his eldest daughter, Matilda.

Henry's daughter Matilda had been married to Henry V of Germany (who died in 1125). In 1126 the barons agreed to accept her as their next ruler. For greater security Henry I married her to Geoffrey Plantagenet, Count of Anjou.

MATILDA AGAINST STEPHEN

Despite their promises to Henry I, many Norman barons were still reluctant to see his daughter Matilda – or any woman – become the next monarch. Many barons did not like Geoffrey of Anjou because he tried to weaken their power. There was also another contender for the throne: Henry I's nephew, Stephen of Blois, son of William the Conqueror's daughter Adela and the French Count of Blois. He was more likely to let the barons have their own way. In the end the rival claims of Matilda and Stephen of Blois seemed to be decided when Stephen was the first to arrive in London after King Henry died in 1135.

Aided by his brother Henry, Bishop of Winchester, Stephen quickly won the support of the Church, and only three weeks after Henry died he was crowned king. Matilda, however, did not give up her claim to the throne.

STEPHEN'S WEAK REIGN

The Normans had provided England with 60 years of firm rule by three strong kings. Stephen, however, was both good natured and weak. Unchecked by a firm king, the Norman barons avoided paying the taxes they owed to the Crown and built castles where they liked, raiding and robbing at random. In total the barons built 100 new baronial castles in defiance of the king. Stephen's disputed claim to the throne also plunged the country into years of civil war. A number of barons went over to Matilda who was supported in her fight for the throne by her half-brother Robert, Earl of Gloucester.

Right: **An impressive Norman castle overlooking its own village, is visited by the king. The lord of the manor or baron was expected to entertain the king and his followers.**

Above: **Matilda was the only daughter of Henry I. Some nobles accepted her as queen in 1141, but most continued to support the weaker Stephen of Blois.**

Above: **Stephen of Blois (1135-1154) was the son of William I's daughter Adela. A weak king, he gained only the contempt of his barons. He was the first English king to allow jousting tournaments.**

- **1110** Henry I betrothes his eight-year-old daughter Matilda to the Holy Roman Emperor, Henry V, and increases taxes for her dowry. Bad weather ruins the crops. Earliest known miracle play performed at Dunstable, Bedfordshire, about this time

- **1114** Henry leads an army into Wales and makes peace. Chichester Cathedral is begun

- **1120** Prince William drowned in the *White Ship* off Harfleur.

- **1121** Henry marries again, to Adela of Louvain

- **1123** Rahere, Henry's jester, founds Augustinian priory of St Bartholomew, London

- **1124** First Scottish coinage

- **1126** Henry persuades barons to accept his daughter Matilda as his heir

- **1128** Widowed Matilda marries again, to Geoffrey Plantagenet, son of Fulk, Count of Anjou. David of Scotland founds Holyrood Abbey, near Edinburgh

- **1129** Fulk goes to Palestine: Geoffrey takes over rule of Anjou, Maine and Touraine

- **1131** Tintern Abbey founded

- **1133** St Bartholomew's Fair first held at Smithfield (the "smooth field"), London; held once a year for over 700 years

Left: **The layout of the castle would include: 1** a spiral staircase; **2** baron's bedroom; **3** great hall; **4** chapel; **5** kitchen and store rooms.

Robert was the illegitimate son of Henry I, but rather than claim the throne for himself he chose to support his half-sister.

THE SCOTS ATTACK

The Scots under King David joined in the fray and invaded northern England in 1138. They were repelled by an English army hurriedly gathered together by the brave Archbishop of York, Thurstan. His troops carried the banners of St Cuthbert, St John of Beverley and St Wilfred, all much revered in the north. The men of the north, led by Thurstan's clergy, fell on the Scots at Northallerton and killed 12,000 of them. This bloody slaughter is known as the battle of the Standard.

MATILDA TAKES POWER

In 1139, Matilda landed at Portsmouth with Robert and they won many campaigns. In 1141 they captured Stephen at Lincoln Castle and imprisoned him at Bristol Castle. Matilda was made queen, and was acknowledged as Lady of the English by Stephen's own brother, Henry, the Bishop of Winchester. But she imposed many taxes on the English people and once again made the barons hostile to her. Her reign lasted only eight months. Bishop Henry deserted Matilda and rejoined Stephen. Robert was captured and exchanged for Stephen. On Stephen's release the war intensified and Matilda was besieged in Oxford Castle. She escaped in 1142 by disguising herself in a white robe and fleeing through the snow. Eventually she went to Normandy, and never returned.

- **1135** Henry I dies in Normandy. Stephen of Blois, his nephew, crosses to England and seizes the throne. Foundation of Fountains Abbey in Yorkshire

- **1136** Stephen gives Cumberland to David of Scotland, who accepts Stephen as king. Matilda claims the throne

- **1137** Geoffrey of Monmouth writes his largely fictional *History of the Kings of Britain*. Stephen wins campaign in Normandy against Geoffrey of Anjou

- **1138** Robert, Earl of Gloucester, begins civil war in support of Matilda. David of Scotland supports her, but is defeated at battle of the Standard

- **1141** Battle of Lincoln: Matilda's forces capture Stephen. Stephen's supporters defeat Matilda's army at Winchester, and capture Robert of Gloucester. Stephen and Robert exchanged

- **1142** Matilda escapes from Oxford Castle

- **1144** Geoffrey of Anjou captures Rouen, and controls Normandy

- **1147** Matilda leaves England

- **1149** Matilda's son Henry returns to England; knighted by David I of Scotland

- **1151** Geoffrey of Anjou dies; his son Henry succeeds him.

- **1152** Eleanor marries Henry of Anjou. Synod at Kells; Pope acknowledged as supreme head of the Church in Ireland

- **1153** Henry of Anjou lands in England. Treaty of Wallingford; Stephen agrees Henry shall be his heir. Death of David I of Scotland; succeeded by grandson Malcolm IV (to 1165)

- **1154** Nicholas Breakspear elected as Pope Adrian IV (only English pope). Death of Stephen

THE BARONS REBEL

With the death of Robert in 1147 Matilda lost her only close ally and so she abandoned her claims to the throne. Stephen was confirmed as king, but he still proved quite incapable of controlling the barons. The country remained in disorder. Stephen tried to gain the barons' support with extravagant gifts, but they realized that he was a weak ruler and that they could do as they liked, which they did.

HENRY OF ANJOU

Order was not restored during Stephen's reign until 1153, when a powerful contender for the throne landed in England. His name was Henry, son of Matilda (Henry I's daughter) and of Geoffrey Plantagenet (Count of Anjou). Henry of Anjou had first come to England when he was 11 years old to be educated in Bristol Castle by Robert of Gloucester who was Matilda's half-brother.

Henry's marriage, in 1152, had surprised Europe. His bride was Eleanor of Aquitaine, ruler in her own right of a large part of France as the heir to the Duke of Aquitaine. Henry's possessions in France were already larger than all England, and now, with his wife, he controlled more than half of France.

In 1153 Henry landed in England to claim his right to the throne. Although he could not defeat Stephen decisively, at Wallingford in Oxfordshire he forced Stephen and the barons to accept his terms to end the civil war. Stephen was to keep the throne, but acknowledge Henry as his heir. Stephen, the last of the Norman kings, died in 1154, and Henry II was crowned King of England.

Above: The four Norman kings. William I and William II are on the top row; Henry I and Stephen are below. The first three kings created strong Norman rule, but Stephen threw it away. Until his reign, Norman rule had helped to develop Britain's economy and end Viking raids.

Left: Geoffrey Plantagenet, Count of Anjou, was one of the first people known to have borne a coat-of-arms. It featured the three lions which still appear on the royal arms of England.

RULERS OF BRITAIN

HOUSE	NAME	REIGN	MARRIED	CHILDREN
WESSEX	Egbert First King of all the English	802 – 839	Raedburh	Ethelwulf
	Ethelwulf	839 – 856	1. Osburh. 2. Judith	Ethelbald, Ethelbert, Ethelred I, and Elfred (Alfred the Great)
	Ethelbald	856 – 860	Judith (his stepmother)	
	Ethelbert	860 – 865		
	Ethelred I	865 – 871		
	Alfred the Great	871 – 899	Ealhswith	Edward the Elder, Ethelfleda
	Edward the Elder	899 – 924	1. Egwina	Ethelstan (Athelstan)
			2. Elfleda	
			3.Edgifu	Edmund I, Edred
	Athelstan	924 – 939		
	Edmund I	939 – 946	Aelfgifu	Edwy, Edgar the Peaceable
	Edred	946 – 955		
	Edwy	955 – 959		
	Edgar the Peaceable	959 – 975	1. Ethelfled	Edward the Martyr
			2. Elfreda	Ethelred II the Unready
	Edward the Martyr	975 – 978		
	Ethelred II, the Unready	978 – 1013	1. Aelfgifu	Edmund II Ironside
		1014 – 1016	2. Emma of Normandy (also married Canute)	Edward the Confessor
DANES	Sweyn	1013 –1014	Gunhilda	Canute
	Edmund II, Ironside	1016	Ealdgyth	Edward
	Canute	1016 – 1035	1. Aelfgifu	Harold I Harefoot,
			2. Emma of Normandy	Harthacanute
	Harold I	1035 – 1040		
	Harthacanute	1040 – 1042		
SAXONS	Edward the Confessor	1042 – 1066	Edith (sister of Harold II)	
	Harold II, Godwinsson (died at the Battle of Hastings)	1066		
NORMANS	William I	1066 – 1087	Matilda of Flanders	Robert, William II, Henry I, Adela (married Count of Blois)
	William II, Rufus	1087 – 1100		
	Henry I	1100 – 1135	1. Edith (Matilda)	William and Adela (drowned on *White Ship*), and Matilda (married Geoffrey of Anjou)
			2. Adela of Louvain	
	Stephen of Blois	1135 – 1154	Matilda of Boulogne	Baldwin, Matilda, Eustace

GLOSSARY

allegiance loyalty to a person or cause

bailiff lord of the manor's chief officer

canonize to formally declare a person a saint. Used by the Roman Catholic Church

besiege to surround a town or castle, cutting off supply lines and attacking with the aim of capturing

Celts Iron Age tribes from Europe

civilization a stage in society when people have developed skills and a way of living together in communities and towns

Holy Roman Empire a federation of European states and princes that lasted from 800 to 1803

hypocaust Roman underfloor central heating system

milecastle fort on Hadrian's Wall – built to station Roman soldiers and officials

monastery residence of a religious male community, bound together by religious vows and living apart from society

mosaic a pattern or picture made of coloured tiles – used to good effect by the Romans on their floors etc

noble person of high birth directly serving the king

pagan a person who follows any pre-Christian religion, especially one with many gods

Picts 'painted people' north of Antonine Wall who periodically harried the Romans

shire county; now only found as part of many county names

slave a person legally owned by another without freedom or rights

Witan the Anglo-Saxon council-meeting of wise men

INDEX

ACKNOWLEDGMENTS

The publishers would like to thank the following for supplying additional illustrations for this book:

Picture research:
Alex Goldberg, Elaine Willis

page 19, Canute; p23, Norman arch; and p29 Norman craft-workers: Mark Peppé

p32, Four Norman Kings:
e t archive